wendell's
guardian angel

bob jones iv

AMBASSADOR

wendell's *guardian angel*
© 1995 Bob Jones IV

ISBN 1 898787 39 5

Published by

Causeway Press
9 Ebrington Terrace,
Londonderry.

AMBASSADOR PRODUCTIONS, LTD.
16 Hillview Avenue,
Belfast, BT5 6JR

Emerald House Group, Inc.
1 Chick Springs Road, Suite 102
Greenville, South Carolina, 29609

list of
contents

if *only* ...!

The airspace over the streets of gold bristled with activity. Angels flew this way and that, hurrying off to their day's activities. Newly trained guardian angels in full armor sped off to protect their clients while angel choirs and angel bands hovered in midair, practicing the day's selections. Musical notes floated on the warm breeze, jumping and rippling like a fountain, then fell lightly onto the grass where they turned to sparkling diamonds.

With all the excitement of a new day filling the air, hardly anyone noticed the lone figure on the ground. Angels, of course, would much rather fly than walk, so the beautiful streets of gold served mostly as a very expensive decoration. For everyone except Avery, that is. Every day he walked the streets alone, watching the other angels trace their graceful patterns across the sky. The tips of his own useless wings, meanwhile, dragged along the street behind him.

He carried a crystal basket in his right hand, and every few steps he'd stop, reach over to the side of the road, and pluck a diamond from the grass where it had fallen. "The choirs are outdoing them-selves today," thought Avery as he eyed his almost-full basket. "There are diamonds everywhere."

He could almost feel one particularly beautiful melody wrap itself around him as he walked. His heart pounded with thanksgiving for all the wonders of heaven; his lungs felt as though they would burst. He watched a beam of light ricochet off the streets of gold, bounce against the pearly gates, and finally break in a thousand glimmering sparks upon the lake of glass. Avery couldn't hold back any longer. He opened his mouth and joined the chorus that echoed around him everywhere.

"Forever, and ever,
Alleluia,
Alleluia!"

It was no good. Avery's notes didn't soar and circle and float to the grass and form diamonds. They just sort of hung in the air for a moment, wobbled uncertainly, then fell clumsily to the street and rolled into the gutter. The problem wasn't with Avery's voice; he knew he could sing. Late one night he had climbed to the top of heaven's highest mountain, almost as high as the angels fly, and sung a magnificent hymn of praise. When the angels awoke the next morning, they were all humming Avery's song and talking about the beautiful voice that had sung that song in their dreams the night before.

No, Avery's voice wasn't the problem. It was the air. Up there - up where the other angels flew - the air was thin and crisp and light. The chirping of a cricket would have sounded like a masterpiece up there. But down on the streets of heaven where Avery walked, the air was much thicker and heavier. "It's like trying to sing in a room filled

with whipped cream," he thought with a sigh and a shrug of his shoulders.

The action of his shoulders made the feathers in his wings rustle. He glanced back at them hopefully. But no, they still dragged behind, as useless as a tail or a couple of extra toes. How he longed to beat those wings and rise effortlessly into the air and join his voice to the angel chorus instead of walking by himself along the unused streets, picking up the diamonds that other angels had made.

If he hadn't been in heaven, where of course there are no tears, Avery would have cried just then. Instead he shrugged his shoulders again and listened to the rustling of his feathers. "My wings are fine," he said to himself. "They're just as good as any other angel's. So why can't I fly like the rest of them?"

By now the music in the air was reaching a climax. A thousand trumpets joined in, blaring their praise. "I've got to learn to fly," thought Avery. "I'm an angel. I *have* to sing." The pounding of five hundred drums swelled the crescendo. "I know I've tried it before, but this time it's going to work." Just overhead the cymbals crashed, crashed, and crashed again. Avery's heart was in his throat. Once more he joined the chorus, belting out the notes as loudly as he could sing them. But with the magnificent music swirling all around him, Avery couldn't even hear his own voice. A bitter sob stuck in his throat as he clamped his mouth shut and watched his lonely little notes roll down the gutter, drop into a drain, and disappear.

• • •

The airspace over the streets of Brookville was heavy with smog. Wendell's eyes itched and watered as he tried to focus on the road they were travelling. "The streets of grime," said Wendell's mother from behind the wheel of the station wagon. "I always said I'd never come back to the streets of grime, and look where I am."

"The streets aren't that bad, Sweetheart. They raised taxes two years ago, earmarked to help clean up ... ." Wendell had stopped listening to the voice coming from the passenger seat. Something else had caught his attention. *Sweetheart.* It had been a long time since he'd heard anyone call his mother sweetheart. His father used to call her that, once. Wendell liked it when his father used that word. It was so warm and safe-sounding.

"Dad," Wendell said without thinking, "why's it been so long ... ." The voice coming from the passenger seat broke off in mid-sentence. Wendell's mother glanced in the rearview mirror, then glued her eyes on the road. The man beside her turned around slowly. "What's that you say, Wendell?"

"Uh, nothing, Grandpa. I mean, I said 'bad.' You know what I mean. Bad. It's uh, too bad we don't get to go to the zoo more often. You and me, I mean."

"Well why didn't you say so," said Grandpa. "We can come as often as you want."

"Great," said Wendell. "Thanks, Grandpa." He settled back in the rear seat and pulled his knees up under his chin. His mother shot him an angry look in the rearview mirror, but he pretended not to see it. Wendell knew better than to talk about his dad. He hadn't meant to; it had just slipped out.

Grandpa started yelling again about all the improvements that had been made in Brookville. Wendell's mother said Grandpa yelled because he was nearly deaf and couldn't hear himself or anyone else unless they shouted. Just now he was yelling something about clean streets and clean air. Wendell just smiled and shook his head. Clean streets? Clean air? Now San Diego had clean streets and clean air, but Brookville was no San Diego. And a zoo! San Diego's zoo was one of the largest in the world, Wendell's father had always told him, and he believed it. There were so many animals in the San Diego zoo, he could never see them all in one day. So Wendell and his father went to the zoo again and again, and every time they saw something new. Now that was a zoo!

San Diego had a zoo all right. It also had friends. Real friends, not a bunch of dumb kids who looked at you like you were from another planet or something. Wendell missed his friends a lot more than he missed the zoo. You could find a zoo anywhere, but friends were only in San Diego. In fact, just last week, Wendell's new class had taken a field trip to the Brookville Zoo, but he had stayed home. He told his mom he was sick, and when she put the thermometer in his mouth and left the room, he wrapped his hands around it real tight to make it hot. Who wanted to go to the zoo with a bunch of dumb kids who weren't your friends?

"When was the last time you went to the Brookville Zoo, Wendell?" Grandpa yelled from the front seat.

Wendell leaned up close to the old man's left ear. "I dunno," he yelled back. "Mom - uh, I mean Mom," he said, lowering his voice, "when was the last time I came to the zoo?"

"Oh, it's been five or six years ago, I guess," she answered. "You couldn't have been more than three."

"Aren't you going to answer the boy's question?" shouted Grandpa, who hadn't heard a word.

Wendell's mother smiled and patted her father's knee. "Sorry, Daddy," she yelled back. "I said, I think it was about five years ago the last time you brought him here. Remember, you and Mother pulled him around the zoo in that red wagon?"

"Sure I remember that," Grandpa answered. He said it softly this time, as if he were talking to himself. Then he started yelling again. "You don't remember that, do you Wendell?"

"Huh-uh," said Wendell, "I was only three."

"Well, you're going to remember this time," Grandpa shouted. "I want you to have a great time so you remember, okay?"

"Sure I'll remember this time, Grandpa. I'm almost nine now. You don't forget stuff when you're almost nine."

Wendell's mother laughed. "Your grandfather's almost 79," she said quietly, just to Wendell, "and he'd forget to eat if we didn't drag him to the table three times a day."

"What's that?" Grandpa shouted.

"Nothing, Daddy," Wendell's mother shouted back. "Look, here's the zoo."

She turned the car past the playground and into the parking lot. Wendell saw some of his classmates from school on the merry-go-round, but he didn't try to get their attention. Instead, he slid a little lower in the seat until his mother stopped the car at the front entrance.

"Okay, Daddy," she yelled as she gave the old man a kiss, "you and Wendell have fun and try not to catch cold. I'll come back for you at about four o'clock, as soon as I'm done with my job interview."

"Right, Sweetheart," he answered. "Hope you're not late for the interview because you gave us a ride. I could've driven myself, you know."

Wendell and his mother just smiled at each other. Grandpa hadn't driven a car in two years. "Take good care of him," she said.

Wendell shut the door and waved as she drove away. "Well, now it's just the boys," Grandpa shouted. "You and me. We're gonna have a great time. First thing we'll do is buy lots of cotton candy and peanuts, so the next time your mother 'drags me to the table,' I won't be hungry at all."

They started walking toward the ticket window. Suddenly Wendell stopped. "Wait a minute, Grandpa," he yelled. "How'd you know Mom said she has to drag you to the table?"

Grandpa never stopped walking. He just looked back over his shoulder, smiled, wiggled his bushy white eyebrows, and motioned for Wendell to follow.

counting *the gold*

By the time the angel choirs finished their singing, Avery was exhausted. He could never remember collecting more diamonds than on this day. The meadows were covered with them, glittering like a million raindrops on the grass after a storm. Avery had carefully stooped to collect each one, knowing that the diamonds he found would eventually be set in crowns for the King.

Each time the crystal basket filled up, Avery would trudge back up the golden streets to the treasury house. The streets wound across meadows, up little hills, through forests and flower gardens, and finally into town, where elegant mansions towered against the blue sky. It was a scenic walk, and newcomers always caught their breath each time they turned a corner to find some unexpected new view. But after a while the surprise wore off, and even the newcomers abandoned the streets, taking to the sky instead.

As an angel flies, the trip from the field of diamonds to the treasury house took hardly any time at all. But for Avery, all alone on the winding street, the way was long and tiring. As he reached the treasury house with his final basket of diamonds, his feet ached and his breath came in short puffs. He pushed against the big oak door, which swung open with a creak.

"Avery, my boy, back again?" called out the treasurer, a jolly fat angel by the name of Julius.

"Back again," puffed Avery as he pushed the door shut behind him. "Four baskets today! You should have heard the angels singing. So many beautiful notes dropping on the grass everywhere - I thought I'd never finish. But I didn't mind," he added quickly, lest Julius should think he was complaining.

Julius looked up from his ledger books and eyed Avery with a funny expression on his great round face. "You *really* didn't mind?" he asked. "Not even just a little?"

Avery blushed. "Well, I tried not to," he answered. "I sang along with the angels some, and listened to the birds, and watched the wind roll across the grass, and picked some flowers, and held each diamond up to the light to see the sun turn into a thousand different colors, and ..." He paused, uncertain if he should go on.

"And?" Julius prompted.

Avery sank down onto a pile of gold coins and rested the crystal basket on his feet. He wanted someone to talk to, but he really didn't know Julius very well. He glanced up at the older angel. Julius was still watching him, but now he was nodding his head, and each time he nodded, his chin disappeared into the fatty folds of his neck. For some reason, Avery decided right then to trust him.

"Uh, where was I? I held the diamonds up to the light to see the sun turn into a thousand different colors ... and I ... I ... watched the other angels fly." Now that Avery had started talking, he didn't want to stop. "They looked so majestic up there, with their white wings beating against the blue sky and their blond hair shining in the sun.

Sometimes they flew so fast I could hardly see them, just a bunch of white and gold streaks tracing patterns in the sky. They looked so important up there, and I felt so small down on the street. Even the birds can fly and sing, but all I can do is walk around and pick up the diamonds that others make."

Avery's words trailed off, and he sat in gloomy silence. He could hear the heavy breathing of the treasurer angel, but he didn't dare to look up at him. Then he heard something else: creaking wood, like the sound the door made. He looked at the door. Still shut. The creaking was coming from the other side of the room. Out of the corner of his eye, he shot a glance toward Julius. He could hardly believe his eyes! The old angel was getting up.

In all the years that Avery had been delivering his diamonds to the treasury house, never once had he seen Julius come out from behind the desk where he sat counting. But now, with great effort, and much huffing and puffing, Julius was heaving his great bulk out of his wooden chair.

Avery held his breath. Was he in trouble? Had he said too much? Angels weren't supposed to complain - after all, what was there to complain about in heaven? A wide shadow fell across Avery, and he looked up again sheepishly.

"Avery, Avery, Avery," Julius said with a shake of his head, which made the fat under his chin flap back and forth. "Such an unhappy angel!"

Avery felt ashamed. "I'm not really unhappy," he said. "It's just that ... ."

"It's just that you're an angel, Julius interrupted, "and angels are supposed to fly. Is that it?"

"Yes," Avery answered, "that's exactly it." With a groan and a wheeze, Julius plopped down on the gold coins next to Avery. Avery thought he could almost hear the gold squealing under the weight.

"You don't like collecting diamonds?" Julius asked.

"I don't mind collecting the diamonds, but they're the praise of other angels. I want to fly so I can sing my own praises."

"Nothing at all wrong with that," Julius said. "You've been the best diamond collector I've ever had, Avery. Tell you what. You take this afternoon off and go back to flying school. I'll collect the diamonds."

"You?" Avery was stunned.

"Sure," Julius laughed. "Obviously I don't get enough exercise." He patted his great stomach to prove his point. "And obviously you don't get enough flying practice. So we both win."

"You mean it?" said Avery, jumping up from the pile of gold coins. "I can spend all afternoon practicing my flying?"

"Absolutely. Just tell the professor I sent you. You can do it, Avery. I know you can fly."

"Thanks, Julius," shouted Avery as he heaved open the big oak door. He paused for a moment. "Julius," he said slowly, "if I do learn to fly, and I get promoted to the angelic chorus, can I still come see you sometimes?"

"Not *if* you learn to fly, Avery - *when* you learn to fly. And of course you can still come see me. In fact, if you don't, I'll have your flying license revoked!"

Avery laughed, waved, and ran out into the sunshine. Julius just sat on the floor among the coins for a moment, feeling good about his own generosity. Then suddenly it hit him: he was too fat to get up! "Avery! Wait!" he shouted. But it was too late; the heavy door had already creaked shut. He settled back among the coins with a sigh. "Exercise," he said to himself. "Julius, you've got to get more exercise."

• • •

Wendell and his grandfather sat at a picnic table just inside the front gates of the zoo. So far the only animals they had seen were a bunch of brightly colored gummi bears. The gummi bears were gone now, as were the chocolate covered peanuts and the Coke. The pink cotton candy was only half gone, but Wendell was ready to leave the concession area and see some real animals.

"You all full?" Grandpa asked.

Wendell nodded. "Yeah. I think I'm gonna get a stomach ache."

"Uh-oh," said Grandpa as he stood up. "You won't tell on me to your mother, will you?"

"Naw," Wendell answered. "Besides, I was the one who picked all the stuff out."

Grandpa wadded up his Coke cup and tossed it toward the trashcan - a perfect hook shot. "You may have picked it out, but I paid for it. That makes me the culprit as far as your mother's concerned. So we'll just let this be our little secret."

Wendell threw his cup at the trashcan too. It fell to the pavement a foot short of the goal. "Come on, Wendell," Grandpa shouted as if he were a block away. "You can make a better shot than that. Are you going out for the basketball team at school?"

Wendell shook his head. "I don't like basketball much," he shouted back as he picked up the cup and tried to throw away the gummi bear wrapper, which kept sticking to his cotton-candy-coated fingers.

"Don't like basketball? Since when? You used to shoot ball all the time."

Wendell was losing his patience with the wrapper. He pulled it off his right-hand fingers, but it stuck to his sticky left hand too. He tried his right hand again. No luck. Finally he tried pulling it off with his teeth.

"Well?" Grandpa shouted again. "Didn't you used to play all the time?"

"Yssh," grunted Wendell, still holding the plastic wrapper between his teeth. He spit it into the trashcan and tried his answer again. "Yes," he yelled, "but that was back in San Diego." Then, too, quietly for his deaf old grandfather to hear, he added, "That was back when I played with Dad."

"Well I don't see why you can't play here, too," Grandpa muttered loudly. "You can play basketball in Brookville just the same as in San Diego."

Wendell didn't mean to hurt Grandpa's feelings. "Sure," he shouted, "I guess I can. If I ever make any friends, maybe I'll start playing ball." He wanted to get off this subject before he had to listen to a lecture about making new friends. Grandpa had just opened his mouth to start the lecture when Wendell saw the balloon man.

"Grandpa," he interrupted before the old man could say a word, "can I get a balloon?"

It worked. Grandpa forgot all about the lecture he was going to deliver and dug into his pocket instead. Wendell took the dollar and exchanged it for one of the silver helium balloons with red letters that said "I Love the Brookville Zoo." He decided to tape the balloon to his San Diego poster when he got home.

"Thanks, Grandpa," he shouted. "Can you hold this for a second while I get the rest of the cotton candy from the picnic table?" He pushed the string into his grandfather's hand and ran back to the table. The balloon would be perfect with the poster, he thought. It would be happy-looking, just like San Diego.

He reached the picnic table and picked up the half-eaten stick of cotton candy. He turned back to his grandfather just in time to see the string float through his fingertips.

"Catch it, Grandpa!" he shouted as he dropped the cotton candy and ran toward the balloon. Grandpa jumped off the ground and swatted at the end of the string, but it was no use. The balloon floated lazily up toward the clouds that always seemed to hover over Brookville.

"Oh, Wendell, I'm sorry," Grandpa said, holding up his crooked fingers. "It's this arthritis, and the string was so small."

"I know, Grandpa. It's okay. I was just gonna tape it to a stupid old poster anyhow."

They started walking toward the monkey cage, Wendell's favorite exhibit. He looked back over his shoulder to watch his balloon rise over the tops of the trees and disappear into the gloomy clouds overhead. "Oh well," Wendell said to himself so Grandpa couldn't hear, "there goes something else I'll never see again."

Grandpa reached out his hand and Wendell held tight to the gnarled old fingers. He decided to roll up the San Diego poster when he got home and put it under his bed, next to the basketball.

at *flight school*

Avery ran the whole way to Flight School without stopping. Past the mansions, up the hills, through the forest, across the meadow: his bare feet galloped along, barely touching the golden surface of the street. As he ran, his eyes scanned the meadow on either side of the street. Not a diamond to be seen. He had done his job well.

When he spotted the brook that babbled along between the meadow and the orchard, Avery suddenly veered off the street and ran through the grass. To his left, a golden bridge spanned the brook, but he didn't feel like using it today. He'd soon be flying, and he wanted to get used to the feeling of the wind under his feet.

The brook loomed just ahead now. He could hear the water gurgling as it bounced and rolled over the smooth white stones in its bed. Avery glued his eyes on the sandy bank that lay on the other side of the brook. That's where he would land, he decided.

The gurgling of the brook grew louder till it combined with the sound of the wind and the pounding of his own feet in the grass.

Thud, thud, thud, thud, thud: his feet and his heart pounded in unison. The steep riverbank was underfoot now; he could feel the dirt between his toes. He opened his mouth, screwed his eyes shut, took one last terrific stride, and then - he was airborne.

For just a fleeting second he was aware of the wind all around him. It whipped through his hair, rustled the feathers in his wings, and blew the dirt from the soles of his feet. In that second he couldn't hear his heart or his feet or even the brook down below. All he heard was the wind whistling in his ears.

"Aieeeeeeee!" yelled Avery. He kicked his feet wildly in midair and beat the wind with his wings. The graceful, beautiful moment was over. He could feel himself falling. He opened his eyes just in time to see the sandy bank rushing up to meet his feet. He had made it!

He landed with a loud "Oomph!" and his feet dug into the sand. As he fell forward onto his hands and knees, he heard a splash behind him. He glanced back to see the tips of his wings bobbing in the water like leaves on a low-hanging branch. Then he jumped up, brushed off his knees and kept running. Who cared about a couple of wet wing-tips? He had just flown over the brook.

"Jumped," something inside him said as he ran through the orchard, his wings dragging in the dirt behind him. "You *jumped* over the brook."

"All right, all right," Avery said to himself, "I jumped over the brook. But it was almost like flying. And by the end of my lesson today, I'll never have to jump again!"

At that thought, he jumped straight up into the air and kicked his heels together. From now on, someone down on the street would have to pick up *his* diamonds.

Avery could see the entrance to the flight school now. The black iron gates loomed just at the end of a row of peach trees. Visions of himself dancing in the sky filled Avery's head as he ran the last few yards toward the gates.

Just outside the gates he ran into the golden street again. He stopped beside the street and wiped his feet carefully in the grass that grew there. It would never do to track dirt from the orchard all over heaven's famous streets of gold. When he was sure his feet were clean, he stepped onto the street and tugged at the bell pull that hung before him.

Avery waited nervously for someone to answer his ring. He let his head fall backward as far as his neck would allow and studied the lettering that formed an arch over the top of the gate. "Professor Flotsam's Flight School," it said. Avery swallowed hard at the sight of that name.

"Well, are you going to stand there gawking all day, or are you going to come in?" Avery jerked his head up so quickly that it made him dizzy. There, standing in the open gate, was Professor Flotsam himself. He looked just like Avery remembered him from the last flying lesson: bony fingers, piercing blue eyes behind gold-rimmed spectacles, a sharp, pointy nose, and that wild shock of white hair that seemed to jump from his scalp in all directions.

"Are you going to come in?" the professor repeated, emphasizing each word.

"Oh, yes, sorry," stammered Avery as he pushed past the professor and through the gate. "I didn't hear you open the gate."

"Of course you didn't hear me open the gate," Professor Flotsam answered. "Did you expect a creaking noise or something? This is heaven, you know. Things don't creak here."

Avery opened his mouth to tell the professor about the creaking door of the treasury house, but then he changed his mind. He liked the creaking door and the creaking furniture and the fat, creaking angel in charge. He hated to think of Professor Flotsam running over to the treasury house and oiling everything - including Julius - so he kept his mouth shut.

The professor didn't seem to expect an answer, anyway. He kept talking a mile a minute, as if he were afraid that every word might be his last.

"No creaking gates in heaven," he repeated. "Can you imagine what would happen if the pearly gates creaked? That would hardly do, would it?" The two of them were walking away from the gate now, toward the practice area.

"Heaven just wouldn't be heaven if things creaked and squeaked and groaned," he continued. "No, my boy, in heaven, everything has to be up to sniff. It wouldn't hurt to learn that little lesson and never forget it. You'll go far as an angel if you remember ... ."

Avery saw that the professor did not plan to pause for air in the near future, so he simply interrupted. "Up to *what?*" he asked.

Professor Flotsam was startled at this interruption. His hair seemed to stand a little more on end. "Up to what? What's up to what?" Then he remembered. "Ah, up to *sniff!*" He bent lower to whisper into Avery's ear. "On Earth they say up to 'snuff,' but of course we wouldn't want angels talking about snuff, would we?"

Suddenly the professor stopped walking. Avery glanced up to see what was the matter, but the professor wasn't looking at him. He was looking over his head.

"Your name is Avery, right?" he asked slowly. It was the first time Avery had ever heard Professor Flotsam say anything slowly.

"Right," he answered.

"Of course that's right. I never forget a name. Avery, did you by any chance walk through an orchard on your way to Flight School? Through the orchard, I mean, instead of on the street of gold?"

Avery could hardly believe his ears. How did the professor know? "Yes sir," he said, because of course angels never lie.

"Aha!" the professor said, still gazing over Avery's head. "And did you wade through the brook instead of using the golden bridge?"

"No sir," Avery answered proudly. "I flew, er, I jumped clear over it!"

"Not *clear* over it," Professor Flotsam corrected him and began walking again. "Your wings didn't quite make it."

Avery looked over his shoulder and groaned. Two dirty little trails stretched all the way back to the gate. His wet wing-tips had picked up dirt from the floor of the orchard and tracked it all over the professor's spotless Flight School!

"I'll clean it up, sir," he promised as he hurried to catch up with the professor. "I'll quit practicing ten minutes early so I can come back and clean it up."

Professor Flotsam had now reached a large round building. He stopped at a door marked Practice Area. "No, my boy, that won't do, will it?" he said. "You must stop twenty minutes early so you cannot only scrub and polish the street, but clean those wing-tips as well. Agreed?"

"Agreed," said Avery. He would have agreed to polish the streets every day for a week, so long as he got to go through that door where the professor was standing.

"Very well," Professor Flotsam said. "You may now enter the Practice Area." He pushed the door open, and Avery followed him through.

The Practice Area still looked just as it had years ago when Avery used to take daily lessons. The round walls were covered with thick foam padding, as was the dome ceiling high overhead. Someone had painted the padding with brightly colored scenes of life on Earth: trains and planes and puppies and pirates seemed to jump off the walls wherever Avery looked. He used to think these pictures were terribly exciting; the green dragon with the long neck that stretched clear to the top of the dome used to terrify him. But that was back when he was a baby angel. The paintings all seemed rather childish now.

Suddenly Avery was embarrassed. As he scanned the room he saw dozens of rosy-faced baby angels with dimples in their chubby knees. He was old enough to be an instructor, but instead he was still taking lessons. Maybe he should just forget it, go back to collecting diamonds.

"No!" Avery stomped his foot to renew his determination. "You want to fly. Julius believes in you. There's no turning back now. Besides, who cares what the others think?"

Aloud he said, "Professor Flotsam, I don't need another lesson today. I know how I'm *supposed* to do it. Is it okay if I just practice some?"

"Certainly, certainly," the professor answered. "Practice makes perfect, you know. There's just one problem, as you can see. We're all out of balloons at the moment."

Avery and Professor Flotsam had now reached an iron railing that formed a large ring in the middle of the room. The floor of the ring consisted of a dark cloud, and above this cloud dozens of baby angels practiced their flight patterns while several instructors flitted here and there, offering advice. A helium balloon was tied around the waist of each student, allowing him to float in midair while he got used to beating his wings. Some of the balloons were plain, while others proclaimed slogans such as Walt Disney World, Happy Birthday, or Vote for Smith.

"Balloons are getting harder and harder to come by," the professor continued, leaning on the iron railing. "Fewer children today are buying balloons, so of course fewer are losing them. Or maybe kids have just learned to hold on tighter. In any case, we're facing a real shortage up here. You can't very well learn to fly without a balloon, can you?"

"Can't you just send a bolt of lightning to scare some little girl into letting go of her balloon?" Avery asked.

"Absolutely not!" the professor answered, waving a bony finger under Avery's nose. "That sort of behaviour is strictly forbidden. We can collect the balloons that are accidentally lost, but we can never interfere. Children on Earth are very fond of their balloons, you know. It wouldn't be right to take them away by force."

Avery was ashamed for his selfish thought. But he was also very disappointed. His precious practice time was ticking away! If he didn't learn to fly this afternoon, he'd be back to collecting diamonds tomorrow.

Then suddenly he saw it. A silver hump was just beginning to push its way up through the cloud. "There!" he shouted. The bottom of the balloon popped into view, followed by a long string. "There! My balloon!"

Professor Flotsam spotted it too. He jumped over the railing, plucked the balloon from midair, and with one flap of his wings was back to Avery. As he tied the balloon around Avery's waist, he gave a few last-minute instructions: "Now remember, no fast flying; flap your wings, not your arms; and watch where you're going. If you need any help, ask one of the instructors on duty. I have to go to do some paperwork. I'm in charge, you know - no time to give lessons."

"All right," he continued as he finished tying the knot and hoisted Avery up over the railing. "You're on your own. You've got three hours' practice time."

He let go, and Avery floated slowly upward. "Thanks, Professor Flotsam," he called. There was not a breath of wind in the Practice Area, so Avery rose straight up toward the dragon's head at the top of the dome. He beat his wings awkwardly, trying to change directions.

"Aieeee!" he yelled, and all the other angels, quietly practicing their flying, stared at him as if he were crazy. But Avery didn't care what they thought. He was free! He was floating! Soon he would get rid of this silver balloon with the red letters that said 'I Love the

Brookville Zoo.' Soon he would fly all alone, faster and higher than any other angel in all of heaven.

"Wheeee!" he shouted, then, "Ooof!" as he hit the padded roof of the dome. He put his feet right in the nostrils of the painted dragon that used to terrify him and pushed off the ceiling. He was free again, floating effortlessly in midair.

Down below, Professor Flotsam blew a note on his silver whistle. "Instructors' meeting," he called out. "Fifteen minutes' free time for all students."

The flight instructors flew quickly to the professor's office, while the baby angels one by one drifted out of the practice ring in search of food or water or someone to change their diapers. Soon Avery was all alone in the air. He closed his eyes, quit flapping his wings, and just enjoyed the feeling of floating. He bounced off the ceiling again, but now he was humming to himself, so he didn't hear the quiet little hissing noise overhead. He just kept his eyes closed and floated.

He could see himself as the lead singer in the heavenly chorus, singing so many perfect notes that it would take two angels to collect all the diamonds. He could almost feel the thin air in his nostrils. His notes would be beautiful indeed! No more of the thick, heavy air that surrounded the streets of gold.

Suddenly he twitched his nose and sniffed twice. The air was incredibly heavy here. His eyes flew open and he saw, not the dragon and the pirates and the iron railing - he saw nothing, just gray all around. Where was he? Then all at once he knew. He was in the cloud! He had sunk through the floor of the Practice Area!

Avery flapped his wings wildly. He flapped his arms, too, and kicked his legs, but nothing helped. He could feel himself dropping, as he had when he jumped over the brook. Now he heard the hissing overhead and looked up at his balloon. It was getting smaller and smaller, shrivelling up like bacon in a griddle.

"Help!" Avery screamed at the top of his lungs. "Professor Flotsam! Somebody! Heeeeeelp!"

a *crash landing* at *the zoo*

"Aieeeeee!" screamed the monkeys in the monkey cage. They screamed as they swung from vines or jumped up and down or beat each other over the head. Some of the little girls standing around the cage clapped their hands over their ears to shut out the noise, but Wendell kind of liked it. It seemed to him the monkeys must be having an awfully good time to make such a racket. He couldn't remember the last time he had screamed out of pure joy and excitement.

"Noisy little rascals, aren't they" shouted Grandpa. No one looked at him funny, because everyone near the monkey cage had to shout. "I remember when you used to run around the house yelling and screaming like that. Your mother just about had to tie you up to put you to bed."

Wendell shrugged. "I'm older now," he said.

"You're not too old to have some fun," Grandpa answered.

"I do have fun, Grandpa. I'm having fun today. I just don't yell and scream, that's all."

"If you're having fun, it wouldn't hurt to show it every once in a while," Grandpa shouted. Wendell was glad for the screeching of the monkeys that drowned out their conversation for the people standing around. Grandpa paused uncertainly. "If you're feeling sad sometimes," he continued, "it wouldn't hurt to show that either."

Wendell could feel Grandpa looking down at him, but he kept his own eyes glued on the cage. He tried to remember the last time he had screamed happily like those monkeys. He had screamed at the baseball stadium when Dad reached higher than all the other fathers sitting around to catch the ball that had popped back foul into the stands. He had screamed again that autumn as he ran around the yard jumping into piles of sweet-smelling leaves Dad had just raked. Was that the last time?

"No," thought Wendell, "it must have been the time I couldn't sleep." He still could remember getting out of bed, walking into the TV room, and catching Mom and Dad kissing instead of watching TV. Even now he could feel the joy that had bubbled up inside him as he laughed and pointed and jumped up and down in the doorway until his father swept him up off the floor, wrapped his big arms around him, and started kissing him all over the face. He had laughed and screamed that night until tears ran down his cheeks and he could hardly breathe. That was the last time he'd seen his parents kiss. "I haven't wanted to scream since then, either," he thought.

Wendell couldn't see the monkeys any more. All he saw were a few brown blurs that seemed to be swimming before his eyes. He shook his head and swallowed hard as he blinked back the tears. He hadn't cried yet, and he certainly wasn't going to cry now.

He tugged at Grandpa's sleeve without looking up. "I gotta go to the bathroom," he said. He started to turn and leave, but felt Grandpa's hand on his shoulder.

"I didn't mean to upset you," Grandpa shouted.

Finally Wendell looked up and smiled at his grandfather. "Naw, you didn't upset me. I just gotta use the bathroom, that's all. Meet you by the elephant area, okay?"

Grandpa nodded and Wendell disappeared around the corner. He ran down the sidewalk past the reptile house and the penguin pool and the ice cream stand until he found the little building marked 'Restrooms.' He pushed through the door and stopped just inside. His heavy breathing echoed in the empty room. He leaned against the cool tile wall and closed his eyes. There was a sob in his throat, but he choked it down and stumbled to the mirror that hung over the sinks.

His straight brown hair, the freckles across his nose, the dimples that were visible even when he didn't smile: everything about his face looked normal except his eyes. They were as red as the taillights on a car, and puffy too.

Wendell turned on the cold water full force and splashed it angrily against his face. "I will not cry, I will not cry, I will not cry," he muttered to himself. His father had been gone for four weeks, and he hadn't cried yet. This was no time to start being a crybaby.

He cupped his hands under the water again, then brought them up to his face. All at once there was a thud on the roof so loud it made him catch his breath. The water went straight up his nose, and he coughed and spluttered like the engine of an antique car.

Wendell shut off the water and studied himself again in the mirror while he listened. The water glistened on his face and dripped off his chin. His eyes, less red now, were wide with surprise. Or was it fright? In the split second after the thud and before his coughing, he was sure he had heard an "Oomph," like the sound someone makes when he gets the wind knocked out of him.

He listened hard, but all he could hear was the gurgling of the drain, the beating of his own heart, and the faint drip, drip, drip of the water falling from his chin. Not a sound came from the roof. He pulled the tail of his tee-shirt out of his jeans and wiped his face dry on it. Then he tiptoed to the door, still listening for any sound from overhead.

The bathroom door squeaked slightly as he opened it, but in the silence it sounded like a scream. Wendell froze and listened again. Still no sound. Maybe he had just imagined the "Oomph." Probably a tree limb or something had just crashed on the roof then fallen to the ground. It was probably ... .

Then he saw it. A balloon hung listlessly over the edge of the pointed roof. *His* balloon. "Don't be silly," he said to himself. "That could be anybody's balloon." Still, it looked like his balloon: silver with red letters that said, 'I Love the Brookville Zoo.' But his balloon had soared into the sky less than an hour ago. This one just hung from the roof and fluttered slowly in the breeze, as if it were tired or disappointed. It looked shrivelled, too. Obviously it had lost most of its helium.

"That *is* my balloon; I'm sure of it," Wendell thought. "I'm going to get it back, too." He ran right under the balloon and jumped as high as he could several times. Each time, the tips of his fingers fell just short of their goal.

He spotted a stick in the dirt and picked it up. It was long and forked like a slingshot. Wendell hoisted the stick over his head and carefully positioned the crook so that it caught the balloon just where the string was tied on.

"This is like fishing," thought Wendell as he pushed on the balloon with his stick. But instead of coming down to the ground in the crook of the stick, the balloon just stopped. Wendell pushed harder. The string went taut and stood straight out behind the balloon, but as hard as he pushed, he couldn't make it budge.

For some reason, Wendell wanted that stupid balloon more then anything just then. There was nothing special about the balloon itself - it hardly even had any helium left - but it was *his*. It had disappeared without a trace and he thought he'd never see it again, but now it was back, and he wouldn't let it get away a second time.

He was getting desperate now. He had been gone to the bathroom a long time, and his grandfather would be waiting for him at the elephant display. But he *had* to get his balloon back. He would have to go up and get it, he decided.

He dropped the stick and looked around for a way to get up on the roof. The cement sidewalk went right up to the front of the little building and met a sheer brick wall. No way up on this side. Wendell stepped off the sidewalk and wandered around the corner. The building was set in a wooded area off the beaten track from the main attractions of the zoo. Trees grew on all sides but the front, providing both a convenient ladder to the roof and a screen that would hide him from others' sight.

Wendell found a good, sturdy tree and began to climb. He kept climbing until he was higher than the edge of the roof, then scooted out onto an overhanging limb and dropped. He landed with a thud and sat down hard on the steep angle of the pointed roof. For a moment he couldn't catch his breath, and he remembered the "Oomph" he had heard in the bathroom.

He dug his sneakers into the shingles to keep from sliding and flipped over onto his stomach. He could see the balloon from here. It still fluttered over the front edge of the roof, but the end of the string was nowhere to be seen. The thin white trail ran along the shingles for a way, then disappeared over the peak of the roof.

He pressed his toes against the roof and started inching his way toward the top. He kept his stomach flat against the surface and pushed himself up with his hands and feet. Just ahead, a ventilation pipe stuck up through the roof. Wendell struggled up several more inches and grabbed the pipe with both hands. From here he could pull himself even with the pipe, plant his feet against it, and crawl just a few more inches to the peak.

Just then he heard voices down below. He held his breath and pressed himself as flat as he could against the roof.

"Look, Daddy," said a little girl's voice. "There's a balloon on the roof. Can I have it?"

"Well, I'll see what I can do, Honey," came a man's voice.

Wendell's stick popped into view beyond the edge of the roof. He watched it maneuver into position behind the balloon and then jerk. The string went as taut as a telephone line, but the balloon didn't budge. After several more jerks, the stick disappeared again.

"Sorry, Honey," came the voice, "it's stuck on something. I'll buy you a new one at the gate."

Wendell heard two sets of retreating footsteps and breathed a huge sigh of relief. The balloon was still his! All he had to do now was reach the peak of the roof. He quickly pulled himself up on the pipe, then clambered higher so he could plant a foot against it. His fingers were almost to the top now. He edged up a few more inches until his fingers closed around the hump at the peak of the roof.

He had done it! As he pulled himself up higher, he could feel something soft brushing against his fingertips, but he didn't even think about it. "I conquered the roof!" he told himself proudly. He pushed again with his toes. "I climbed the mountain!" The top of his head was now even with the peak of the roof. "I scaled Mount Everest!" One more inch and he would be able to see what his balloon was stuck on. "I beat the ... ."

Then suddenly he couldn't think any more. Everything around him started to spin. He felt a cry welling up inside, but it wouldn't come out of his mouth. All at once he knew why the balloon wouldn't budge. All at once he knew what the soft feeling at his fingertips meant. All at once he was looking directly into the wide blue eyes of an angel.

only *1000 years old?!*

"Hello!" the angel whispered with an embarrassed grin. "I, uh, I think I'm stuck up here." Wendell's lips moved dumbly, and his tongue felt as thick as the soles of his Nikes. He wanted to talk, but he wasn't sure what an eight-year-old boy was supposed to say when meeting an angel.

"See, I was taking these flying lessons," the angel continued, "but my balloon ran out of gas and I fell out of flight school and landed here. Where's here, anyway?"

"You're in the Brookville Zoo, Sir," is what Wendell wanted to say, but his rubber tongue just wouldn't cooperate. He only managed to force out a single word: "Zoo," he whispered hoarsely.

"A zoo!" replied the angel. "That's great! Can we see the dragons while I'm here? I used to be afraid of dragons, but that was when I was just a little kid. I'm not afraid of them any more. In fact, when I hit the ceiling today in Flight School, I put my feet right in the dragon's nostril's, flapped my wings, and ... ."

The angel flapped his wings to emphasize his point. Suddenly Wendell's head was surrounded by zillions of white feathers and a great rush of wind. He was so surprised by the sudden, powerful action that he forgot to hang on. He lost his grip and started to slide down the steep roof.

At last Wendell found his tongue. "Yooowww!" he yelled as he skidded downward. His shirt, which he had untucked to dry off his face in the bathroom, rolled up as he rolled down, and his bare stomach scraped along the rough shingles. He tried desperately to apply the brakes with his tennis shoes, but gravity was stronger than his rubber soles. His right foot hit something and bounced off as he continued to slide. The ventilation pipe!

A moment later it flashed by his eyes. Wendell waved his arms desperately, trying to catch hold. The fingers of his left hand felt cool metal, and he clamped them shut around it. He jerked to a stop like a yo-yo that has reached the end of its string. For a moment he just hung there, clinging to the pipe and trying to catch his breath. His stomach felt as if someone had stuck a thousand needles in it. He wanted to touch it and see if it was bleeding, but he didn't dare let go of the pipe.

"Pssst!" came a whisper from the other side of the roof. "Are you okay over there?"

"Yeah," Wendell called back, "I think I scraped up my stomach, though."

"Shhhh!" the angel whispered again. "Do you want everyone to know we're up here? Come back over to my side and I'll see what I can do about your stomach."

Wendell winced as he started to climb slowly back toward the peak of the roof. Instead of pressing flat against the shingles this time, he humped his back to keep from scraping his stomach any more. Still, with each move he felt a sharp pain, and the climb to the top seemed endless.

When his fingers at last closed over the tip of the roof, there were tears in Wendell's eyes. He blinked them back angrily before pulling his head into the angel's view. Now that he could see the angel again, he forgot all about the pain in his stomach. Wendell had never seen a more beautiful creature. The angel seemed to shine from the inside, causing his white robe, blond hair and blue eyes to glow warmly. He had the face of a child and was smaller than Wendell, and when he smiled - as he was just now - Wendell could feel the glow spread to his own body.

"Come on over," the angel whispered. "Let me take a look at that stomach."

Wendell obediently threw his leg over the peak of the roof, flipped over onto his back, and lowered himself down beside the angel, who was holding onto another ventilation pipe. Then angel hooked his elbow around the pipe and reached out to raise Wendell's blood-stained tee-shirt with his free hand.

"Hmm," the angel said, "sorry about that. I'll try not to flap my wings any more. Mind if I fix it?"

Wendell was too dumbfounded to speak, so he just shook his head. The angel smiled again and laid his hand on the scraped-up place. As Wendell watched, the hand on his stomach began to glow more brightly than before. Slowly the glow spread from the hand to his stomach, like a sunrise breaking over the horizon. Wendell let his head fall back against the shingles. He could *feel* the glow creeping ever wider through his body. There was no more pain in his stomach, just a warm, tingly feeling.

"All better," the angel announced.

Wendell opened his eyes and raised his head with a start. Was it over already? He looked down at his stomach; perfect white skin stretched from the top of his jeans to the bottom of his tee-shirt, with not a cut or a scrape to be seen. "Wow," Wendell said, "thanks ... ." He paused as he realized he didn't know the angel's name.

"Avery," said the angel. "My name is Avery."

"Thanks a lot, Avery - er, Mr. Avery." Again Wendell was confused. How were you supposed to address an angel? "Thank you, Sir," he said. That didn't sound right, either, so he tried again. "Thank you, Your Majesty - Your Highness - Your Holiness ... ."

Avery's laugh sounded like a mixture of falling water and silver bells. "Just Avery," he said. "I'm only a thousand years old, much too young to be a 'Mr.' or a 'Sir.'" He saw the look of shock on Wendell's face and added quickly, "That's very young for an angel, you know, because we never die. My friend Julius, the treasurer angel, is a million years old. He was around before your planet was even here. I wonder what the guardian angels did back then, before there were any men around who needed guarding." Avery fell silent as he pondered this important new question.

"Avery," Wendell ventured after a few moments of silence, "what are you doing here?"

"Like I said," Avery answered, "I was taking flying lessons at Professor Flotsam's Flight School, when my balloon lost its helium and I sank to Earth. I've been holding onto this pipe ever since. Do you think you could help me down off this roof?"

Wendell ignored the question. There was something else he had to know. "Angels fly with balloons?" he asked.

Avery blushed a deep red. "Well, not all angels. See, they use balloons in Flight School so you can get used to floating in midair. Then once you learn to fly, you don't need your balloon any more." He paused for a moment, then continued. "The problem is, I never learned to fly." He said it very quietly, and Wendell thought the glow inside his new friend was not as bright as before.

"Come on," Wendell said, "let's get you off this roof."

Avery brightened up immediately at the thought of getting his feet back on solid ground. Wendell scooted down the roof on his bottom until he was directly underneath Avery, then leaned back so his shoulders touched the roof. "Okay," he whispered to the angel, "put your feet on my shoulders and let go of the pipe."

Avery obeyed, and the boy and the angel inched down the roof with the silver balloon following behind. "Whoa, that's it," Wendell whispered when they reached the edge of the roof. "Dig in your toes for a minute while I find a tree to climb down." Wendell spotted a branch hanging out over the roof. He grabbed ahold and quickly lowered himself to the ground.

"Okay," he called quietly, "climb down the tree like I did."

"I *can't* climb down the tree," came the answer.

"Sure you can," Wendell said. "I do it all the time, and I'm only eight."

"Have you ever tried climbing a tree with wings attached to your back?" Avery whispered loudly.

Wendell thought for a moment about the difficulties that would cause. "Okay," he said, "you're right. Just let yourself fall and I'll catch you."

Avery was not too fond of that idea. "Are you sure?" he asked.

"Sure I'm sure," Wendell said. "I'm right underneath you, and you're smaller than I am. No problem, just come on."

Wendell waited. Silence. He waited some more. Still no sign of the angel. "Avery," he said at last, "are you coming or ... ."

Suddenly he was interrupted by a shriek. "Aieeee!" yelled Avery as he made up his mind and let himself fall. Wendell held his breath and stretched out his arms. He hoped he really was directly underneath the angel. He glued his eyes on the edge of the roof just over his head and waited.

All at once a white bundle burst into view and bounced off the edge of the roof. Wendell took a step back and opened his mouth to holler instructions, but it was too late. For a moment Avery seemed to be frozen in midair, arms, legs, and wings flailing wildly. In the next instant, all was pandemonium as boy and angel hit the ground and rolled along in a tangle of blue jeans, feathers, and string. When they finally stopped, Wendell found himself flat on his back. Avery was on top of him with one wing wrapped around his head.

"Wow!" Avery said. "That was great. Can we do it again?"

Wendell just groaned and shook his head. He sat up quickly at the sound of footsteps running toward them. A moment later, a tall, thin figure in dark green clothes appeared from around the corner of the building. He wore black sunglasses, and his thin lips did not smile. "Zookeeper," proclaimed a patch on his chest.

"What's going on here?" asked the man. Once again, Wendell found he could not speak. He looked first at the man, then at the angel in his own lap, then back at the man again. How was he going to explain this?

"I said what's going on here?" the man repeated, taking another step forward. Wendell gulped and opened his mouth to explain that the angel had fallen from heaven. Just then he felt a tug at his sleeve.

Avery was right at his ear, trying to whisper something. Wendell strained to catch the words. "He can't see me," the angel said. "His eyes are bad. Just pretend like I'm not here."

Wendell looked back at the man towering above him. Sure enough, he didn't see a hint of surprise on the man's face, only anger. His mind raced to think of an explanation. Then out of the corner of his eye, he spotted the balloon. That was it! He could just tell the truth.

"Well, Sir," he began, "when I came out of the bathroom, I saw this balloon hanging from the roof." He held up the balloon to prove his point. "I had lost a balloon just like it earlier today, so I really wanted this one bad. I couldn't reach it, and I couldn't knock it down with a stick, so I climbed up on the roof to get it. I guess you heard me get

off the roof just now." Wendell laughed to show that it was all in good fun and he hadn't intended any harm.

The zookeeper didn't laugh; he didn't even smile. He just stared for a moment, then said, "Where's your father?"

Wendell hated it when people asked him about his father. 'I don't know," he answered quietly. He felt Avery's hand on his shoulder; the angel seemed to understand. "My name is Wendell, and I'm here with my grandfather. He's going to meet me at the elephant area."

"Well, you get back there right now, and don't ever let me catch you here alone again. Understand?" the man snarled.

"Yessir," Wendell answered, but the man had already turned and stalked away. Wendell just stared after him for a moment, until his thoughts were interrupted by Avery's sigh. As he looked back at the angel, he remembered a question he had. "Avery," he asked, "why did you say the zookeeper couldn't see you?"

"Because he has very bad eyes," Avery answered. "Only people with good eyes can see angels. Now I have a question for you: why do you feel so much pain when you mention your father?"

Wendell didn't answer directly. "I felt your hand on my shoulder," he said, "and I knew you understood. How did you know what I was feeling?"

Avery shrugged. "I'm an angel," he said. "What do you expect?" He saw that Wendell's curiosity wasn't satisfied, so he continued. "Humans listen only to the *words* of others, but your words don't always say what you really mean. For instance, when the man with the bad eyes asked where your father was, all you said with your voice was, 'I don't know.' But I was listening to your heart, and it said, 'I miss him so much it hurts inside, and more than anything in the world I want him to come back.'"

"My heart said all that?" Wendell asked without looking at the angel. "I'm sure glad no one else can hear my heart."

"Oh, but they can," Avery said. "Anyone who really loves you can hear what your heart is saying. When did your father leave you?"

"Just a month ago. That's when we moved to Brookville. Mom didn't want to be alone." Wendell fell silent. Pipes squeaked inside the building as someone turned on a sink. "I don't want you to listen to my heart any more, Avery," Wendell continued. "I don't even listen to my heart any more."

He tried to get up, but Avery restrained him. The angel laid his hand on the boy's chest. Again the warm feeling began to spread. But this time, instead of creeping outward from the angel's hand, it went straight down - down into Wendell's heart.

"I didn't *try* to listen to your heart," Avery said. "It was crying so loudly, I couldn't help but hear."

By now the warm feeling had filled Wendell from his Adam's apple down to his waist. For some reason he wanted to sing. Instead, he jumped up with Avery still in his arms. He hoisted the angel onto his shoulders and started around the corner of the building, dancing as he went.

"Where are we going?" Avery asked.

"To find the elephant area," Wendell answered. "I can't wait for you to meet my grandfather. He won't be able to see you, because he wears glasses, but you're gonna like him." Wendell danced out onto the sidewalk with the angel bouncing on his shoulders. He hadn't felt this good in a long, long time. He felt like he could fly.

an *elephant experience*

The boy and the angel followed the sidewalk through a maze of cages and pens containing every kind of animal imaginable. Avery laughed and pointed and bounced excitedly on Wendell's shoulders each time he saw an animal that he recognized from the walls of the Flight School. Wendell entertained his new friend by imitating the sound each animal made. He barked like a seal, grunted like a gorilla, and even roared so much like a lion that Avery nearly fell off his shoulders from laughing so hard. A light rain had begun to fall, and all but a few stragglers had already left the zoo in search of drier amusement.

As the pair rounded a building marked 'Zoo Office,' the elephant area suddenly loomed just ahead. It was a huge display complete with trees and cement cliffs and even a little waterfall. Three old, gray elephants lumbered around within the iron railing.

Avery was thrilled. He had heard stories about these magnificent creatures, but since there were no elephant pictures at Flight School, he had never actually seen one. He scrambled to his feet on Wendell's shoulders, clinging to the boy's hair to keep his balance. "Wow!" he said. "They're as big as a house. They're even fatter than Julius. They're beautiful!"

Wendell winced as the angel's heels dug into his shoulders. He turned to look for Grandpa, but the old man was nowhere to be seen. "I've gotta find my grandfather," he said to Avery. "You coming?"

"Can I stay and watch the elephants?" Avery asked. "I promise not to leave until you get back."

"Oh, all right," Wendell said. "I'm just gonna run back toward the bathroom and see if Grandpa went looking for me. I'll be back in a second." He lowered Avery onto a bench next to the iron railing to give him a better view, then ran back down the deserted sidewalk in the direction of the restrooms.

•   •   •

Wendell walked back to the elephant display slowly, his hands shoved into the pockets of his jeans. Grandpa was nowhere to be found, and Wendell was beginning to feel guilty. He'd been gone for a long time, and Grandpa was sure to be worried and angry.

As he approached the zoo office, his thoughts were interrupted by wild trumpeting from the elephants. It sounded like a large marching band playing out of tune, and for some reason it made Wendell nervous. "You should never have left Avery alone," he told himself as he broke into a run.

He rounded the corner of the building, and his eyes swept the green bench where he'd last seen his friend. No sign of Avery! He stopped in his tracks and scanned all around the iron railing - nothing. What if someone had found Avery alone and kidnapped him? What if another angel had come and whisked him back to heaven? "I didn't even get to say goodbye ..." Wendell thought.

Just then an elephant bellowed again, long and loud and high. Somehow it reminded Wendell of the excited screaming of the monkeys when they were having a good time. A light dawned in Wendell's mind. "The elephants are having *fun*," he thought, and that could only mean one thing - Avery!

He jumped onto the green bench to get a better view. At first he could see only a mass of wrinkled gray skin and big, floppy ears. The three elephants were huddled together, stomping their feet, swaying from side to side, and occasionally raising their trunks to the sky to let out a terrific bellow. Then, in the midst of the gray, Wendell saw a flash of white. He craned his neck for another look.

One of the elephants moved a few steps away, and suddenly Wendell saw him. There, swinging from the tail of the middle elephant, was Avery. His white robe and feathers flapped in the breeze as he swung like Tarzan on a living vine. "Aiieeeee!" he cried with his head thrown back and his eyes closed against the wind in his face. All three elephants responded by throwing back their heads and blowing another piercing trumpet call. Wendell could have sworn the wrinkled old creatures were smiling from tusk to tusk.

"Avery!" he cried, trying to make himself heard over the elephants' trumpeting. "Avery, get back out here." It was no use; Avery couldn't hear a thing over the ruckus. Wendell watched as Avery shimmied up the elephant's tail and climbed onto its back. He turned cartwheels the whole way up the creature's spine until he stood at last on the elephant's head between two great, flapping ears.

The elephant loved it. Rearing back on its hind legs, it let out the loudest, longest trumpet blast yet. Avery lost his footing, slipped from his perch, and broke his fall by grabbing the nearest available object - the elephant's ear.

The other elephants reared up on their hind legs too, bellowing at the top of their mighty lungs. Wendell thought he should be angry, but he had to laugh. Who could be mad when the elephants were having so much fun?

Suddenly the cry of the elephants changed. Wendell could sense the difference, though he wasn't quite sure why. Somehow the joy was gone from the elephants' voices, and in its place was - pain.

The elephant on the right moved several feet to one side, and at last Wendell understood. On the far side of the display area stood the zookeeper Wendell had met earlier. He held a thick canvas hose, like the kind firemen use. A high-powered stream of water shot from the end of the hose, blasting the middle elephant right in the belly. The creature, still balanced on its hind legs, staggered backward in pain.

The zookeeper's angry voice broke over the frightened cries of the elephants. "Shut up, you stupid beasts," he yelled. "You gimme a headache." He advanced a few steps closer to the iron railing, driving the jet of water still harder into the elephant's tender stomach.

Wendell looked on, horrified, as the old, gray creature reeled back clumsily. He thought he could see the hurt and confusion in the elephant's eyes. Then suddenly those eyes were looking right into his, and he forgot the chaos around him. It was just boy and elephant, and the elephant's deep brown eyes seemed to be begging, "Please help me. It hurts. Please do something; do something; do something."

"DO SOMETHING!" With a shake of his head, Wendell snapped out of his trance. That final cry was no dream! From his precarious

perch on the elephant's head, Avery, too, was begging for help. "Make him stop, Wendell," the angel cried. "I can't hold on."

Still Wendell stood rooted to his spot, his mind and his heart racing. "What can I *do?*" He wanted to help, but how could he stop the grim, unsmiling man with the firehose? He could see the elephant losing its balance now, tottering like an old man in a strong wind. Then, as if in slow motion, the creature began to fall. Wendell opened his mouth to scream, but no sound came out.

Dimly, as if it were a thousand miles away, Wendell heard Avery's voice: "Put your feet in the dragon's nose, Wendell!" Then the angel's voice stopped as the old elephant crashed heavily to the ground.

"Put my *what?*" thought Wendell. Then he remembered. He closed his eyes and tried to envision Avery putting his feet right into the nostrils of the painted dragon that had once terrified him. "But there are no dragons on Earth!" he thought.

He opened his eyes and looked at the elephant. The huge gray animal lay on the ground now, looking like a whale that had somehow washed ashore on a lonely beach. The joyous trumpeting of the elephants had stopped, replaced by a heavy silence. Still the zookeeper fired a steady stream of water into the fallen elephant's belly. The creature just lay there, unable to move, kicking its legs slowly. One floppy ear was spread along the ground, and under it Wendell could make out a single white wing, bent at an impossible angle.

Wendell felt anger building up inside him like a slow burn. "How dare that man ..." he thought. His gaze travelled along the stream of water back to where the zookeeper was standing. Avery's last words still rung in his ears: "Put your feet in the dragon's nose, Wendell." Right before his eyes, the zookeeper seemed to change. No more did Wendell see the man in the green jumpsuit. Instead, he saw a monstrous dragon holding the firehose. Flames leapt from the dragon's nostrils and along his back were rows of razor-sharp scales.

The fire inside Wendell began to die. Surely he was no match for the dragon! But then he saw something else: the dragon's mouth was turned up in a kind of crooked, hideous smile as he continued to blast the helpless elephant. "He's enjoying this!" thought Wendell, and the slow burn inside suddenly boiled over. "He *enjoys* torturing that old elephant." The dragon dissolved away, and once again Wendell saw the green-clad zookeeper, his lips still twisted into a smile.

"Stop it!" screamed Wendell. The strength of his own voice surprised him, so he tried it again. "Turn off the water!"

The zookeeper looked up, startled, and saw Wendell for the first time. He stared at the boy for a moment, then turned his attention back to the elephant lying on the ground. Instead of turning off the water, he advanced still closer to his prey until he was leaning over the iron railing to get the best possible shot.

Wendell jumped from the bench and charged in the direction of the zookeeper. His heart was pounding in his ears, but he hardly noticed. The zookeeper didn't even bother to look at him, so absorbed was he in his little game.

Wendell cut wide in order to approach the man from behind rather than from the side. For a moment the green shirt disappeared again, replaced by the deadly scales of the dragon. "Too late to stop now," he thought briefly. He screwed his eyes shut and launched himself at the dragon's back with a scream.

The zookeeper reeled under the surprise attack. The weight of the boy on his back forced his stomach into the railing, knocking the wind out of him. He dropped the hose at last, and the jet of water sprayed harmlessly against the back wall of the cage.

The zookeeper's hands were free now, and he groped for the arms of the boy that were wrapped around his throat. Wendell could feel his grip being pried loose, so he wrapped his legs around the man's midsection, planting his heels firmly in the stomach of the green shirt.

The zookeeper stumbled backward clumsily. Unable to shake Wendell off, he backed into the wall of the office that stood nearby. Wendell's breath was forced out of him with a whoosh. The impact jarred loose his hold around the zookeeper's midsection, but he managed to maintain his chokehold around the man's neck.

"Put your feet in the dragon's nose, Wendell." Again the words echoed in his ears. "I'm not in the right position for that," thought Wendell, "but I'll do the next best thing." He reached out and pinched the zookeeper's nose so hard that his reflecting sunglasses clattered to the wet pavement. With a cry of rage, the man backed up against the wall again, harder than before. Wendell's head hit the brick with a crack. He dimly remembered seeing the old elephant rise shakily to its feet, and then there was only blackness.

a *lesson learned*

Wendell found himself surrounded by fire-breathing dragons on a San Diego beach. As the dragons advanced toward him, his father suddenly dropped from the sky and began kicking each dragon squarely in the nose. As Wendell watched the dragons drop dead one by one with a terrible nosebleed, he was suddenly grabbed from behind by a green, scaly paw.

"Help!" he screamed as the dragon began to lick him with a tongue like sandpaper. "Dad, the dragon's got me!"

Having disposed of all but the one remaining dragon, Wendell's father had knelt in the sand to wipe the blood from his penny loafer. When he saw his son in the dragon's clutches, he sprang to his feet and advanced toward the beast. With a confident smirk he reared back and kicked the dragon's shin as hard as he could.

"Yooooowww!" he cried as he fell back on the sand clutching his right foot. "Wendell, I stubbed my toe."

The dragon chuckled and began licking Wendell like a lollipop again. "Dad, do something; the dragon's gonna eat me," Wendell said panic-stricken. His dad simply shrugged his shoulders and turned to walk away.

"Where are you going?" Wendell screamed again. "You can't just leave me here."

"Sorry, Son," his father called back without turning around. "It's too hard. I tried, but it's just too hard."

Wendell couldn't believe what he was hearing. "You didn't try! You gave up! You gotta put your feet in the dragon's *nose*, Dad, not kick him in the shin."

His father simply shrugged his shoulders and continued to walk away. Suddenly Wendell's mother appeared in the clutches of the dragon's other paw. She looked so small and frail compared to the beast that held her. Wendell wanted to help her, but he couldn't move.

"Please come back, Honey," she cried. "Wendell and I can't do this by ourselves. We need you."

Still the man walked slowly away, never turning back. Just ahead of him a swirling mist began to form. Wendell was crying now. The salty tears ran down his cheeks, dropping onto the green scales of the dragon's paw, where they sizzled and turned to steam. "Please don't give up now, Dad," he managed to choke out. "I need you. You can't just walk away."

The crashing of the waves on the beach drowned out Wendell's words. His father had reached the edge of the mist now. It swirled around him, seeming to draw him in. "Dad!" Wendell screamed one last time before the white fingers of mist closed around his father, hiding him from view. His mother bowed her head silently, but Wendell could see her shoulders shake. He looked back to the spot where his father had disappeared, but there was only nothingness. Wendell tried to call again, but his body was racked by a sob. "Dad?" It was just a whisper this time, a whisper that the moaning wind picked up and carried off to sea.

•   •   •

Wendell opened his eyes and sat bolt upright. He was on a dingy gray couch in some kind of office. He looked around wide-eyed for the dragon, but all he saw was a desk, a filing cabinet, a coat tree - and Avery. The little angel was kneeling on the dirty carpet beside the couch.

"Where am I?" Wendell asked. Even in his own ears, his voice sounded choked and unnatural. He put his hands to his face and found his cheeks wet with tears. He lay back on the couch with a groan. "I've been crying in my sleep, haven't I?" he said, staring at the ceiling.

Avery nodded. "You started to cry as your father disappeared into the mist."

"I told you not to listen to my heart any more," Wendell said. He didn't feel angry, just empty.

This time the angel shook his head. "I didn't have to," he said. "You were talking in your sleep. Besides, you should have cried a long time ago instead of storing it all up inside."

"My dad said only sissies cry," Wendell said. "Guess I'm a sissy."

Avery reached for the boy's chin, turning his head so that the two were eye to eye. "You put your feet in the dragon's nose," Avery said. "That zookeeper was bigger than you, but you didn't let that stop you. You did the right thing even though it was hard. Some people never learn that lesson ... ."

Wendell completed the angel's unspoken thought. "My father never learned that lesson." There was a moment of awkward silence. The low voice of the zookeeper could be heard from the next room. Wendell looked down to avoid Avery's steady gaze. "I hate him," he said at last.

Again Avery shook his head. "You want to hate him because he hurt you and your mother, but you really can't, can you?" Wendell didn't answer, so Avery continued. "Instead of hating him, you just refuse to let yourself need other people. You needed him, and he disappeared into the mist, so you're never going to need anyone again. That's how you feel, isn't it?"

Slowly, Wendell raised his eyes to meet his friend's gaze. His voice was a hoarse whisper. "He never even said goodbye. I just woke up one morning and he was gone." The words spilled out faster and faster now. "Mom was sitting on the couch in her bathrobe with her knees pulled up under her chin and her eyes were all red and she looked a hundred years old and all she could say was, 'I'm so sorry, Wendell.'" Again the tears were coursing down the boy's cheeks, but he plowed on with his story. "I put my arms around her neck, but she felt hard like stone and her cheek was cold and she just kept saying over and over, 'I'm so sorry, Wendell,' and I wanted to hate him so much but I just can't." The narration ended with a long sob and again the room was quiet.

Avery let go of Wendell's chin and moved his hands up the boy's cheeks. "That's right," he said. "You go on crying and let me wipe the tears dry." With his thumbs he pressed Wendell's eyelids closed. "Now," he said, "forget about that scene and think of something nice that happened with your father."

For a moment Wendell could see only the gray beach and the swirling mists of his dream. Then slowly his mind filled with a golden glow. No, it wasn't a glow, it was the autumn sunset over a San Diego beach. There were no dragons, not even people. Wendell and his dad walked along the deserted beach hand in hand, picking up shells. Wendell spotted a large, beautiful conch shell just at the edge of the tide and ran to pick it up. He washed his treasure off in the cool, shallow water and ran back up the beach to show his dad.

The shell was white and heavy and nearly as big as Wendell's own head. Here and there little spines seemed to burst out of the shell's smooth surface, pointing upward like miniature church steeples. Wendell hoisted his prize overhead so his dad could have a closer look. "It's a beauty, huh?" he asked proudly.

His father patted his shoulder. "Biggest one I've ever seen," he said.

Wendell examined the shell up close, turning it over and around in his hands. "What's it for, Dad?" he asked.

"It used to be a fish's house," his dad answered.

Wendell was puzzled. "Why would any fish leave such a beautiful house?"

The man didn't answer right away. Wendell looked up at his father, silhouetted against the golden sky, gazing out to sea. "I don't know," he said at last. "Maybe it was too small, and the fish needed more room to move around. Or maybe it just got too heavy for him and he needed a rest - it would be hard work to drag something like that around, you know."

Wendell looked at the abandoned house again. The sunset made the wet, white surface of the shell glitter like solid gold. Wendell thought it must be the most beautiful thing he'd ever seen. "Do you think the fish could find a better place than this?" he asked.

His father sighed and looked back down at his son. "Probably not," he said. "Sometimes you just don't know how good you've got it. I imagine that fish is probably sorry he left his home. I imagine he'll never stop missing it."

"I feel sorry for him," said Wendell, looking at the golden cathedral in his hands. "I don't think that fish is very happy away from his home."

This time his father said nothing. He just reached down, scooped Wendell up in his arms, and kissed him on the forehead. Then he hoisted him still higher, over his head and onto his broad shoulders. Wendell held the big shell against his chest and bounced along the beach on his father's shoulders listening to the pounding surf and the sound of the distant traffic. From up here, he seemed to be a part of the sunset, bathed in its golden glow.

He felt that glow spread through his body. The weight of the shell on his chest made him happy, and he clutched it tighter to him. But instead of the hard, wet surface, his touch was met by soft skin. The beach faded away and he once again saw the sights of the little office. He was lying back on the couch, and Avery's hands rested on his chest. Even in the dingy office, Wendell still felt the warm glow of the sunset. He looked into the angel's blue eyes and smiled.

"I guess I should feel sorry for him," he said quietly. "He's not happy, is he?"

Avery shook his head. "Even then, in the back of his mind, he knew he couldn't be happy away from you. Now he's like a little fish in a very big ocean with no shell to go home to."

"Maybe he'll come back home one day," Wendell said.

"Maybe he will," Avery agreed. "Maybe one day he will."

Wendell squeezed the angel's hands. "Thanks, Avery," he said. "Now we'd better get out of here and go find Grandpa." He got up off the couch and headed for the door.

"Forget it," Avery said, "I already tried the door. The zookeeper has you locked in here. I came in through the window, and that's how we'll get you out."

With Avery in the lead, the two tiptoed to the window that stood open over the desk. Suddenly Wendell stopped short. In the silence he could hear more clearly the voice of the zookeeper coming from the next room.

"How long do you think ivory prices will stay this high?" he asked. There was a long silence, and Wendell realized that the man was talking on the phone. Finally the zookeeper spoke again. "Three months? I don't expect any of these elephants to die within three

months. Maybe I can arrange a little *accident* for one of them."
Silence followed again, followed by harsh laughter. Then: "Yeah,
cyanide poisoning is slow and natural; no one will suspect anything.
I promise you'll have the tusks while the price of ivory is still high."

Wendell's head was spinning; he couldn't believe his ears. "Come
on!" whispered Avery, who was already halfway out the window.

"Avery," said Wendell, "he's going to kill one of the elephants and
sell its tusks! We gotta get out of here and tell Grandpa."

Avery put his finger to his lips. Approaching footsteps could be
heard on the other side of the locked door. Wendell ran for the
window at the sound of a key in the lock. Avery dropped out of sight
and Wendell clambered onto the window ledge. The door swung
open. "Stop!" yelled the zookeeper just as Wendell released his grip
and fell to freedom outside the office window.

on *the run*

A light but steady rain had been falling for some time now, and the rubber soles of Wendell's tennis shoes squeaked as he ran along the wet pavement. The zoo appeared all but deserted; even the animals had taken refuge inside their cages.

The boy and the angel had dropped to the pavement on the far side of the zoo office, away from the elephant area. Wendell wasn't sure what lay in this direction, but he knew that somewhere behind them was the zookeeper, and so he kept running. Avery padded along beside him, his soft leather sandals making barely a whisper. For the first time since he'd landed on the roof of the restroom, he was beginning to feel homesick for heaven. It had never occurred to him that he ought to be worried; he was an angel, after all, and angels never die. But what if ... .

Wendell's voice interrupted his thoughts. "You know, Avery," he puffed without breaking his stride, "you better hope we find Grandpa before the zookeeper finds us, 'cause if we don't, you may *never* get back to heaven."

Avery seemed not to hear. "Let's rest a minute," he said. "In there!" He pointed to the open door of the Reptile House just ahead, and they ducked inside.

They found themselves in a big room filled with glass cages. Wendell peeked back out the door to make sure the coast was clear, then sank down onto the cold linoleum floor beside Avery. For a while neither spoke as they tried to catch their breath. Avery broke the silence.

"How did you know I was worried about getting back to heaven?" he asked in a whisper that echoed eerily through the empty room.

"Maybe I listened to your heart," Wendell answered.

"Oh," said Avery, looking pleased. Wendell's conscience began to bother him.

"Okay, so I didn't listen to your heart," he said. "I guess I just knew how I felt, and I thought maybe you were thinking about the same things. So you *are* a little bit worried, huh?"

"A little bit. I've been thinking - there's only one way for me to get back to heaven, and that's for you to tie me up to a whole bunch of helium balloons and then let me go. Since all balloons from Earth end up in Flight School, I'd be home in no time. But if that zookeeper catches you and we get separated, well ... ."

"Can't you do some magic or something?" Wendell said. "You know, turn the zookeeper into a worm or a fly?"

Avery sighed. "You've been watching too much television, Wendell," he said. "Do I look like a wizard to you?"

Wendell studied his friend carefully. The rain had turned the angel's golden curls to a dark brown and plastered them against his forehead. The white robes that had once shone so brightly were now smeared with mud and speckled here and there with long, gray elephant hairs. The strap of his left sandal had ripped loose, and a dirty smudge ran from the bridge of his nose to his right ear.

"No," Wendell answered at last, "you don't look like a wizard. You look more like a drowned rat. We *gotta* get you home."

"Right!" said Avery. The prospect seemed to fill him with some of his old energy. He waved his hands excitedly as he spoke: "All we have to do is find your grandfather, get some money, buy a dozen balloons and send me on my way. Then I'll send an angelic army to take care of that zookeeper, and everything will be ... ."

He stopped in midsentence. Wendell wasn't listening to a word he was saying. The boy was staring at the floor, winding one wet shoelace tight around the tip of his index finger. Wendell finally noticed the silence and looked up, startled. He met Avery's clear, blue gaze for a moment, then looked back down at the floor.

"What's the matter?" Avery asked gently.

"I dunno," Wendell said. The tip of his finger was beginning to turn blue from the pressure of the shoelace.

"Do you want me to listen to your heart again?"

Now it was Wendell's turn to sigh. "No. It's just that - well, you know. You're leaving, just like my dad. Why does everyone have to leave?" He yanked his finger from the shoelace and smacked the floor angrily.

"Wendell, I'm an *angel;* angels belong in heaven. You know I can't stay in Brookville."

"Then why can't I go to heaven with you?"

"Because," Avery said slowly, "you're a little boy, and you belong here. We weren't all made to play the same role, Wendell. You could have been an angel and I could have been a boy, but that isn't the way it happened. Besides, there are no zoos in heaven."

"Yeah, but there are no angels on Earth," Wendell broke in. "Look, Avery, you're not gonna make me feel any better, so let's just drop it, okay? You're gonna leave - fine, I can handle it. I always do." Wendell's chest was heaving now, and his words came in short bursts.

Avery reached out his hand and rested it against the boy's chest. Wendell closed his eyes for a moment and drew a long, unsteady breath. Then suddenly he swatted Avery's hand away and jumped to his feet. "I don't want your help any more, Avery." He was yelling now, his words spilling out in a rush that bounced off the bare walls and hard floor. "I don't want your magic spells or your cheap tricks. Who's gonna make my heart glow when you're gone, huh?" Avery, his eyes wide with surprise, scooted backwards across the floor. Still Wendell continued his assault. "Sure, you can fly back to heaven where everything's perfect and just forget me, but I'm stuck here. Well, as far as I'm concerned, you're already gone. I don't see you, I don't hear you, and I sure don't *need* you."

At last Wendell seemed to run out of words. He just stood there, fists clenched and lips moving dumbly. Then, with a very loud squeak of wet rubber on linoleum, he pivoted 180 degrees, ran out the door, and disappeared.

For a moment, Avery couldn't move. He sat pinned to the floor, Wendell's stinging words still beating against him, wave upon wave. "Perhaps he'll come back," Avery thought, staring out the door. But the cold, gray drizzle outside the Reptile House continued to fall without interruption. Sitting all alone in a little puddle on the floor, Avery couldn't control the shiver that ran up his spine, uninvited.

Suddenly there was the blur of a human figure running from right to left past the open door. "Wend ..." Avery started to call, then bit his tongue. Wendell had disappeared to the left, so that couldn't have been him coming from the right. And there was something else: Avery was sure he had seen a flash of dull green. "The zookeeper!" he thought, jumping to his feet.

He ran to the door just in time to see the zookeeper turn the corner by a hot dog stand. Avery ran after him, his short legs pumping furiously. Although it was difficult to see in this weather, Avery managed to keep the back of the green shirt in view. Beyond that he couldn't see much of anything, but he was certain the zookeeper must be following Wendell.

The zookeeper reached a fork in the sidewalk, hesitated for a moment, then turned left. As Avery approached the fork, he glanced at the sign that stood where the sidewalk split. "Bear Exhibit" read the sign pointing to the left; the other pointed right and proclaimed, "Big Cats." He turned left after the zookeeper, then stopped suddenly. The pounding of his heart seemed louder than usual. He held his breath and listened. He heard the zookeeper's retreating footsteps, the beating of his own heart - and something else.

"That's Wendell's heartbeat!" he said to himself. It seemed to be coming from the right, somewhere off the sidewalk. Avery plunged into the shrubbery that lined the pavement. Almost at once he tripped over something crouching in the bushes. "Wendell!" he whispered as he picked himself up and brushed himself off. "Come on, let's get out of here."

For a moment Wendell didn't move. Finally he raised his head and looked at Avery with red eyes. "Why'd you come after me?" he asked.

"Because I saw the zookeeper following you," Avery said. "Now let's go before he finds out you didn't go that direction."

"I wouldn't have followed you if you said those things to me. That was really stupid, Avery. I'm sor ... ."

Avery clapped his hand over the boy's mouth and held a single finger to his own lips. His head was cocked to one side, and he seemed to be listening. "The zookeeper stopped running," he said quietly. "What lies beyond the bear exhibit?"

Wendell tried to remember the zoo map he'd examined earlier in the day. "Nmphg," he muttered.

"What?" asked Avery looking down at him again. "Oh, sorry," he said, removing his hand from Wendell's mouth.

"I said 'nothing.' I think the bear exhibit is a dead end."

"Then he'll be coming back any minute," Avery said. "Let's go." Wendell jumped up to follow his friend, then ran into his back as the angel stopped suddenly.

"What's the matter?" Wendell hissed.

"Why am I leading?" said Avery. "I've never been here before."

"Oh yeah," Wendell said. "I'll lead. Where should we go?"

"If I knew that, I'd lead," Avery answered.

Wendell looked at his watch. "I know," he said, "it's almost time for Mom to pick us up. We'll head for the entrance and find her before we find Grandpa."

"Great," said Avery. "Let's go."

Wendell hesitated. "Wait a second," he said. "Which way is the entrance?"

Avery shrugged and rolled his eyes. "I don't know. I didn't come in that way, remember?" He held a finger to his lips again and listened. "He's coming back this way," he whispered. "We have to go right now."

"I've got an idea," said Wendell, taking Avery's hand. "Come on!" They broke out of the brush and onto the sidewalk, on the right. But instead of following the pavement, Wendell led Avery across the sidewalk and back into the trees on the other side.

"Where are we going?" Avery asked.

Wendell answered without stopping. "The zookeeper will be looking for us on the sidewalk, so we'll stick to the trees. If we head a little to the left, I think we'll get back to the entrance." The two turned and continued running, the sound of their steps muffled by the wet vegetation underfoot.

Avery squinted through the mist-shrouded trees. Something different lay directly ahead, but he couldn't make out just what it was. A few more steps and they practically bumped into it - a long, gray wall about five feet high. They stopped and leaned against the wall, panting.

"What is it?" Avery asked.

"I dunno," said Wendell, "kind of a funny place for a wall, right in the middle of the forest." Suddenly he brightened. "Wait, I know. It must be the back wall of the zoo!" He ran his hands along the smooth surface of the painted cement wall, thinking. "We don't need to go to the front entrance, Avery," he said. "We can just climb over here, get outside the zoo, and follow the wall around to the front. The zookeeper will never look for us outside the zoo grounds."

"Are you sure?" said Avery. "What if ...?" But Wendell wasn't listening. He had already found a tree growing close to the wall and begun to climb. The wall wasn't much taller than Wendell, but water on the slick, gray paint made it impossible to find a foothold. Instead, Wendell shimmied out on a low branch that stretched just over the top of the wall. He hung upside-down like an opossum, using only his hands and feet to inch headfirst toward his goal.

When he reached the wall, he let go with his feet and sat down on top of it, facing back toward Avery. "Okay," he called to the angel, "your turn."

"We've already been through this," Avery said. "I can't climb trees with these wings on my back. You go find your mother and then come back for me. The zookeeper can't see me anyway, remember?"

Wendell shook his head. "No way. This is a big zoo, and I might never find this spot again. It's now or never, Pal. I know - I'll push this branch down as far as I can. You jump up and grab on, then I'll let go of the branch and you can reach the wall." He started to scramble to his feet.

"But ..." said Avery.

Wendell raised his hand. "No arguments," he said. "Besides, you can't come all the way to Earth and miss out on tree-climbing. Bet you don't climb trees in heaven, do you?" he asked as he pushed down on the branch until it was scraping the top of the wall.

Avery jumped for the branch but missed. "In heaven," he answered as he coiled for another attempt, "most angels fly *over* the trees, so who wants to climb?" Again he jumped and again he fell short.

"Sure, but if you can't fly," said Wendell from his perch on the wall, "you can at least be the best tree-climber in heaven. You'll be the envy of all the other angels. Now try again."

Avery rolled his eyes, tensed the muscles in his legs, and sprang straight up. This time he felt bark under his fingertips and clamped his hands shut around the branch. "Yee-ha!" Wendell whooped. "Now hang on." The boy released his grip on the branch, and it bounced back into place with Avery still hanging on.

Avery's eyes were clamped shut, so he didn't see what happened next. Wendell, startled at the rush of wind and leaves from the bouncing branch, took a little half-step to regain his footing. But his wet tennis shoes found nothing to grip on the smooth, slick surface of the painted wall. He could feel himself falling backwards; he spun around in the direction of the fall. In a split second he saw, not the backside of the zoo, but a long, grassy pit bordered on the far side by an iron railing. The zookeeper leaned on the railing, a horrified look on his face. As Wendell's hand closed around a thin, leafy twig, he saw something else: several cement caves were built into the back of the pit, and in shadow of the caves, something seemed to pace slowly. The frozen moment ended with a snap. The twig broke, and Wendell tumbled into the pit gripping a fistful of leaves.

tussle *with a tiger -* and *home again*

"Aaiiieee!" cried Avery as he bounced up and down with the branch. "Wendell, this is great! You have to teach me how to climb...." He broke abruptly as he opened his eyes at last. "Wendell?" he called uncertainly.

The branch had almost stopped its swinging now; there was only a faint tap-tapping sound as the outermost twigs brushed the spot on the wall where Wendell had stood.

"Wendell?" Avery called again, louder this time. "Come on, Wendell, you can't just leave me hanging here. You know I can't climb trees." Still there was no answer from his friend. Avery drew a deep breath to call again, then held it. A low moaning reached his sensitive ears. It seemed to come from beyond the wall. He cocked his head to one side, trying to listen more closely. There were more sounds now, a sort of confused, disjointed gibberish. "Oops! Whoa, sorry about that. Hang on, Avery."

"That's definitely Wendell's voice," Avery thought, "but he doesn't sound like himself." The angel began to inch slowly, hand over hand, along the branch toward the wall. The upper tips of his wings banged him in the ears as he swung awkwardly from side to side. "Now I remember why angels don't climb trees," he said to himself, rolling his eyes.

Suddenly Avery noticed that the babbling had stopped. He stopped, too, trying to listen more closely. At first he heard only a ringing in his ears, thanks to the beating they had just taken from his wings. But then there was something else: Wendell's quick, shallow breathing - a pant, almost.

"Wendell," he cried again, "are you all right?" Again no answer came; instead, Avery heard only a kind of gurgling sound from beyond the gray wall. He gritted his teeth and started forward again, faster than before. He recognized that sound. He'd made it once himself when Julius had found him sleeping instead of collecting diamonds. The great, fat angel had towered over him, demanding an explanation. Avery had opened his mouth to explain, but in his fright all he could force out was that low gurgle.

He was nearly within reach of the wall now. His aching arms felt as if they would give out at any second. "Don't fall now," he told himself, looking between his swinging feet at the ground far below. "You'll never get back up here." He stopped momentarily to catch his breath. He thought he could hear his shoulder joints creaking, like the sound Julius made when he heaved his great bulk out of the chair.

"Avery!" The cry cut through his reminiscences. It was high-pitched, panic-stricken. Avery swung into action again, forcing his tired arms to respond. At last he could reach the wall. He kicked toward it, trying to find a foothold, but his sandal skidded off the wet surface.

Another scream came: "Somebody help!" Avery moved forward another inch and swung his legs again. This time the heel of his left sandal hooked over the top of the wall and held. Using his foot as an anchor, he pulled himself to the end of the branch then dropped to his seat on top of the wall.

His eyes took in everything at a glance: Wendell sprawled on the grass, too afraid to move; the zookeeper frozen next to the railing on the far side of the pit; and the form pacing slowly back and forth in the shadow of the cave.

Wendell's wide, frightened eyes met the angel's. "Do something!" they begged. But Avery, too, was rooted to his spot. Wendell had fallen into a pit dug much deeper than the land all around. Avery's head swam as he looked down the sheer, seemingly endless face of the wall to where his friend lay almost directly below.

Suddenly, out of the corner of his eye, he glanced a movement in the shadows. The dark form, which had been pacing back and forth, was now walking straight toward them. A few more steps and it emerged from the shadows. Even in the dull light, the gold and black stripes seemed to shimmer. The muscles in the creature's shoulders bulged and then relaxed in rhythm with its slow, graceful steps. Even from a distance, the beast made Wendell seem small and helpless. Its green, unblinking eyes were fixed on the boy as it advanced.

Avery thought it must be one of the most beautiful - and danger-ous - creatures he had ever seen. "What is it?" he called to Wendell without taking his eyes off the beast.

"Tiger!" the boy managed to force out in a choked whisper.

Avery remembered the sign back where the sidewalk split: "Big Cats" it had said. At last he understood. Instead of heading for the entrance, they had somehow run nearly parallel to the sidewalk and found, not the back of the zoo, but the back of the tiger pit.

Still Avery stood transfixed by the beauty of the big cat. The tiger opened its mouth to reveal two rows of gleaming white teeth and a pink tongue that snaked out lazily to wet its lips. It advanced silently, gracefully, its movements almost hypnotic as it stalked closer and closer to its prey.

Suddenly Avery snapped back to reality at the sound of a cry. "Wendell!" It was a desperate voice, one that he had never heard before. Avery looked toward the zookeeper, startled, but the man in the green uniform was looking at someone else - an old man running along the iron railing.

"Grandpa?" Wendell called uncertainly, looking quickly from the tiger to his grandfather and then back again. "Grandpa, I can't move. My ankle hurts so bad!"

Avery saw the old man run both hands through his thick, white hair. Behind the gold-rimmed glasses, there was desperation in the man's eyes. He turned to the zookeeper. "Do something!" he implored. "Get my grandson out of there." The zookeeper, still speechless, could only shrug his shoulders helplessly.

As the old man turned his gaze back toward Wendell, he caught a glimpse of Avery standing on the wall. "You're his guardian angel," he yelled. "Why don't you *do* something?"

"I'm not a guardian," Avery said, hanging his head. "I'm just a diamond collector who accidentally fell to Earth because I can't fly ... ."

"I don't care who you are," Grandpa interrupted. "That's my grandson down there!"

Wendell, too, looked over his shoulder toward Avery. There was the look of a hunted animal in his eyes, and his bottom lip trembled a little, but he didn't say a word. For his part, the zookeeper could only stare dumbly at the empty spot on the wall above the boy's head where everyone seemed to be looking.

The tiger had crept noiselessly to within a few feet of Wendell. With one leap the beast could have been on him, but it was in no hurry. Instead, it turned slightly to the right, circling the boy without ever taking its eyes off him.

Avery saw Wendell's knuckles turn white as he dug his fingers into the grass and dirt. The tiger tightened its circle, coming ever closer,

closer. Wendell scooted back a few inches then winced and grabbed his ankle. He looked back up to meet the steady green eyes of the tiger, just inches from his own.

Avery couldn't breathe. The blood pounded behind his face and roared in his ears. He saw his friend's eyes lock into those of the tiger and his shoulders go slack. Still the tiger closed in slowly on its prey. From the corner of his eye, Avery saw the old man throw one leg over the iron railing. The zookeeper ran to his side, trying to pull him back. But the big cat never flinched. It circled closer, the end of its tail flicking Wendell's back. Saliva dripped from the left corner of its mouth, making a dark spot on the knee of Wendell's jeans.

Fear tightened like a vise around Avery's lungs, squeezing all the air out. The whole world was in blackness now, except for Wendell and the tiger. He saw the beast's whiskers brush the freckles on the boy's face. The cat was behind Wendell now. It stopped. The boy closed his eyes and lowered his head slowly.

Avery jumped. He hadn't planned to; it was just a reflex, like blinking the eye when sand gets in it. With one flap of his wings he bore down on the tiger and the boy. Wendell never saw him coming. For a moment Avery felt the cat's hot breath on his neck, and he felt sick. Then Wendell was in his arms and he was soaring heavenward, away from the terror down below. The boy didn't open his eyes; slowly, his trembling lips curved to a smile, and he wrapped his arms around Avery's neck.

The angel's white wings beat against the sky, carrying the pair high above the cages and the trees and the hot dog stands. The wind whistled around Avery, making his robes swirl and snap. He let his head fall back as he hovered effortlessly in midair, soaking up the weak rays of the sun and slowly breathing in the light, clean air.

"Wendell!" The call from far below broke the magical moment.

"That's Grandpa," Wendell said, opening his eyes at last. "He's worried about me up here." He looked into Avery's eyes for a

moment, then glanced down to where his grandfather was standing. "Whoa!" he yelled. His mind reeled. Grandpa and the zookeeper were barely-visible specks far below. The whole zoo spread out beneath him, along with the parking lot and the highway and even downtown. Wendell tightened his grip around Avery's neck, forcing the angel's face into his chest.

"Wendell, I can't breathe," Avery tried to say, but with his mouth pressed hard against the boy's shirt, all that came out was "Wmph, cp brph." Slowly, the two began to sink toward Earth. They barely drifted at first, then gradually gained momentum, falling faster and faster.

The wind whistled in Wendell's ears; he felt like he was going to lose his lunch. "Do something, Avery!" he said.

But Avery, at the moment, was more worried about suffocating than he was about falling. He could feel himself turning blue as his lungs cried out for oxygen. He struggled to free himself from Wendell's grip, but fright had made the boy strong for his size. Avery knew he would faint soon without air: it was now or never. "Sorry, Wendell," he thought, then opened his mouth and bit the boy hard in the chest.

"Yooow!" screamed Wendell. Instinctively, his hand released its grip on the angel and flew to the burning spot on his own chest.

Avery threw his head back with a long, loud gasp. Immediately the fall was broken, and the pair hovered again in midair, only inches above the trees now.

"What did you do that for?" said Wendell, still rubbing his chest.

"Would you rather we crashed?" countered Avery.

Wendell looked sheepish. "Sorry about that," he said. "I hope you've had your rabies shots, though," he added with a grin.

"What's a rabie?" Avery asked.

"Never mind," Wendell said. "I'm sure you're safe. Can we get down now?"

Avery nodded and flapped his wings. The boy and the angel glided gracefully down toward Grandpa. Wendell saw the zookeeper let go of Grandpa's arm and start to dash away. "Let's get him, Avery!" Wendell said, pointing excitedly.

But Avery didn't even hear him. The joy of flight had so completely filled him that all he could hear was the wind in his ears and the song welling up in his heart. They were just a few feet above the ground now, and the sidewalk sped along below them like the racetrack below the wheels of a dragster. Avery imagined himself back in heaven, skimming along above the streets of gold while some other angel gathered his diamonds. The thought was too much; he couldn't hold back any longer.

"King of kings!" he sang out at the top of his lungs. "Forever and ev...." The song ended abruptly as he crashed to the grass along the sidewalk.

In the next moment there was another crash. A huge, round figure in billowing white robes with about 20 balloons floating above him fell heavily from the overcast sky - right on top of the zookeeper. He lay still for a moment, then, with much grunting and groaning, heaved himself to his feet and brushed the dirt off his robes. He looked down at the still form on the sidewalk and shook his head, causing the layers of fat under his chin to wiggle uncontrollably.

"Oh dear," he groaned, "I seem to have squashed a human. I tried to tell Professor Flotsam that 20 balloons wouldn't be enough!"

Wendell recognized the newcomer from Avery's description. "Julius?" he asked uncertainly.

The big angel saw Wendell and Avery for the first time. "Avery, my boy!" he called out happily as he advanced toward them. "You have no idea how worried we've all been about you. Why, Flotsam closed down Flight School for the first time in 2,500 years so I could have all the balloons I needed to come find you. Of course," he added, "it

turns out that all the balloons in heaven weren't enough to keep me in the air!"

Wendell couldn't help but laugh at the sight of this huge butterball of an angel waddling towards them with 20 helium balloons bouncing along behind like some strange, multicolored tail.

"Don't worry about the damage you did to the man in green," Grandpa said. "He was in big trouble as it is."

Julius stopped suddenly at the sound of Grandpa's voice; he hadn't seen the old man before. "You can, er, see me too?" he asked, surprised. "Does everyone on Earth have such good eyes, Avery?"

Wendell spoke up before Avery could answer. "Wait a minute - Grandpa doesn't have good eyes. He wears glasses."

Julius broke into a deep, rumbling laugh that set his fat quivering. "But of course that has nothing to do with it," he said. "Your grandfather's eyes are good because your grandfather is a good man. It's the wicked, selfish, hateful people who have truly bad eyes."

Finally Wendell understood. "Hey, Grandpa, that's why you could see Avery up on the wall and thought he was my guardian angel!"

Julius found this incredibly funny. "What? Avery - a guardian angel? Oh dear me, wait until I tell Professor Flotsam. My dear boy, Avery is one of my favorite angels in all of heaven, but he's no guardian! Why, to be guardian, an angel must be big and strong and very, very brave. And of course, he must be able to ... ." He paused for a moment and looked at Avery sprawled on the ground with Wendell still halfway in his arms. "Well, you know," he finished quietly.

Wendell scrambled to his feet. "But Avery is brave, Julius!" he cried. "He jumped off the wall to save me from the tiger even before he knew he could fly. How many guardians would do that?"

Julius stared unbelievingly at the little angel in the grass. "Avery *flew?*" he asked.

"Yep," interrupted Grandpa, "he swooped right down there and snatched my grandson from the jaws of death. We're mighty grateful to that young angel, Sir."

Julius looked to Avery for an explanation. "Well?" he said.

The question was met by silence. Wendell suddenly realized that his friend hadn't said a word since their bumpy landing. He glanced toward Avery and found him staring forlornly at the ground, playing with the broken strap of his sandal. Instinctively, he pushed his tennis shoe toward the angel's hand. Avery absent-mindedly stuck his finger through the loop in the shoestring and wound it tight around his finger.

"Well?" Julius pressed on. *"Can* you fly, Avery?"

Avery didn't answer until his fingertip was a deep blue. Finally he let out a long sigh. "Sure, I can fly," he answered. "As long as I have plenty of air in my lungs. But as soon as I run out of oxygen, I drop like a rock."

"Avery, that's wonderful!" Julius said, his fat face breaking into a smile.

"Yeah, right," Avery said. Wendell could see his friend's fingertip beginning to throb. Without a word he gently untwisted the shoelace, freeing Avery's finger. The angel pulled his knees up under his chin. After a moment he said, "I didn't want to fly just for the sake of flying. I wanted to fly so I could *sing.* How am I supposed to sing if I have to hold my breath?"

"Maybe you just aren't *meant* to sing, Avery," Julius said. "That doesn't make you any less important than any member of the heavenly chorus. It just means that there's something else you're supposed to do. Something even more important, maybe."

Wendell interrupted excitedly. "Yeah I remember just a few minutes ago a friend of mine - my *best* friend - told me that we all have a different role to play. My friend had all the answers then," he added.

Avery hung his head. "But why do I have to be a second-class citizen? Why do I have to be the only angel in all heaven who can't fly?"

"I beg your ... the only ... do you really think ... oh, Avery!" Julius spluttered. "What ever made you think you're the only angel who can't fly? Why do you think I floated - er, crashed - to Earth strapped to a bunch of balloons?"

Avery's head snapped up, his eyes wide. In his disappointment he hadn't even stopped to consider Julius's mode of transportation. "*You* can't fly, Julius?" he asked incredulously. "Why didn't you ever tell me that before?"

Julius shrugged. "You never asked, and angel's don't complain. It never occurred to me that you thought you were the only angel who couldn't fly. Avery, my boy, why do you think I count the gold? And who do you imagine cleans the streets of gold and polishes the pearly gates? Can you imagine what heaven would be like if every angel sang in the heavenly choirs?"

"But you knew how much I wanted to fly," Avery pressed on. "Why didn't you tell me that maybe I wasn't meant to?"

"Because every angel, just like every human being, has to find his place. I didn't know for certain that you couldn't fly; indeed, it turns out that you *can*. Would you have kept trying if you thought it was impossible?"

Avery shook his head.

Again Wendell interrupted. "Right! And then you wouldn't have come to Earth and you wouldn't have met me and I would ... never ... have ... ." His voice trailed off and he looked uncomfortably from Grandpa to Julius. "I wish I were alone," he thought, "so I could tell Avery how glad I am that he came to Earth."

Grandpa cleared his throat. "Uh, Julius, do you think I could have a word with you in private?" he said as he started walking away. Julius, looking a bit confused, followed. Grandpa looked back over his shoulder and winked at Wendell, who was watching in disbelief.

"See," Avery said, "I told you that anyone who cares about you can listen to your heart. Now what was it you wanted to say?"

Suddenly Wendell felt foolish. "Can't you just listen to my heart?"

"Sure, but then when I'm gone back to heaven you'll wish you had told me. You never got to tell your father goodbye, remember?"

Wendell nodded. "I um, I guess I just wanted to say that if I had never met you, uh ...." Wendell's mind was searching desperately for the unfamiliar words. He rolled his eyes and stared at the leaves of a tree overhead. "What I mean is, I'm really glad you came, 'cause I understand a lot of stuff now that I didn't understand before. And I really like having you here and you're my best friend and all, but I think even when you leave it's gonna be better than before you came."

Wendell plopped back down on the ground beside Avery without looking at him. The words tumbled out one on top of the other with barely a breath in between them. "You know before, I wondered who would make my heart glow when you're gone? Well, I think I know - I think you will. 'Cause see, it's glowing right now and you're not touching me. It glows every time I think about you, and I'll be thinking about you a lot, so I guess I'll feel pretty good most of the time. So see I understand that you have to go back to heaven, and I'm happy for you 'cause I want you to be happy. And you've made me real happy and I'll go on being happy when you're gone, so I guess what I really want to say is just ...." At last he paused for breath and looked at Avery before finishing his speech with a single word: "Thanks," he said quietly.

Avery felt something tickling his cheek. He reached up to brush the pesky insect off his face, but instead he felt something wet under his fingertip. "Aaagh! What is it?" he asked, his eyes wide. "Am I sick?"

Wendell gave a short laugh. "It's just a tear, Avery."

"But I'm *an angel,*" Avery answered. "*Angels* don't cry."

They both jumped at the sound of Julius's voice above them. "That's just because there are no tears in heaven. Since you're on earth, of course, it's perfectly all right." Avery laughed with relief and tried to dry his eyes. "Sorry to startle you," Julius continued, "but we've really got to be getting back. Professor Flotsam is babysitting for twenty little angels who want to practice their flying. Are you ready to go?"

Avery looked toward Wendell, who nodded with a little smile. "Go on," he said. "You don't want to keep the professor waiting."

"Of course, I'm going to need your help," Julius said to Avery as he and Wendell got up. "Can you hold your breath
long enough to pull me back up to heaven?"

"Sure!" Avery answered. "As long as I don't break into song or scream with excitement, there's no problem."

Now Julius turned to Grandpa. "What will become of him?" he said, nodding toward the zookeeper who still lay unconscious on the sidewalk.

"Don't you worry about it," Grandpa answered. "I've been coming to this zoo for over forty years, so last year they put me on the board of directors. Sort of makes me his boss, doesn't it? I'll see that he gets what's coming to him."

"Wow!" said Wendell. "You're on the board of directors? That's so cool! Can you get them to buy some polar bears?"

Grandpa laughed and patted Wendell's shoulder. "We'll see what we can do," he said.

Avery cleared his throat uncertainly. "Uh, Julius," he said, "Remember you said that every angel has to find his place? Do you really think that I'm too small to be a guardian?"

Julius seemed to consider this carefully. "Well," he said slowly, "I suppose if you can fly, and you've proven your bravery ..." - both Wendell and Grandpa nodded - "then there's no reason that you shouldn't start going to Guardian School instead of Flight School. I'll put in a recommendation as soon as we get back. Of course, it's hard work. You have to learn to drive runaway cars and put out fires and stop bullets and the like - not an easy job."

"I'll learn anything I have to," Avery promised, "and I'll learn it faster and better than any other angel in school." He paused for a moment and knit his eyebrows in thought. "You said my role might be even more important than the heavenly chorus," he continued. "Well, I think I know now what it is. I want to request to be a guardian - *Wendell's* guardian."

Wendell's eyes lit up. "Yeah!" he said. "That'll be great. Give me five!"

Avery looked at Wendell's outstretched hands, confused. "Never mind," Wendell said, giving his friend a clip on the shoulder instead. "Guess you don't do that in heaven."

"Fine," said Julius, "it's settled. I'll recommend Avery to Guardian School as soon as we get back. Which has to be *right now*," he added.

There were handshakes and goodbyes all around: Grandpa shook Julius's hand, Julius shook Wendell's hand, Avery shook Grandpa's hand. Finally Wendell and Avery were left looking at each other awkwardly. Wendell held out his hand stiffly, but Avery reached right by it, laying his hand instead over the boy's heart. "Keep that till I come back," he said quietly. Wendell nodded without a word.

"Well," Julius said loudly, "I suppose that's that. Avery?"

The little angel turned and grabbed ahold of the knot that secured the balloons to Julius's waist. "Thanks for everything," he said with a final look toward Wendell. "Ready, Julius?" The fat angel's nod set his whole body quivering once more. Avery opened his mouth, took in a great gulp of air, and flapped his wings. He rose a few feet off the ground and the balloon strings went taut. Julius, down below, remained anchored to the ground. Avery's eyes bulged and he pressed his mouth into a determined grimace, flapping his wings harder still. Slowly, almost imperceptibly at first, Julius began to rise.

"Go Avery!" Wendell cheered.

"You can do it, Avery!" added Grandpa.

The two angels were above the trees now and rising faster all the time. Julius, looking like a great catch on a fisherman's line, waved at the two figures below while Avery strained heavenward. Wendell shielded his eyes to watch their ascent. In another moment they had burst through the low-hanging black clouds. Their sudden exit seemed to blast a hole in the overcast skies, allowing a little circle of sunlight to penetrate the gloom. Grandpa winced in the dazzling light and turned his head away.

"Feel the glow, Grandpa?" Wendell asked with his face upturned.

Instead of looking at the sky, Grandpa looked down at the boy bathed in sunlight. He rested his gnarled old hand on his grandson's shoulder, which felt high and straight and strong. "Yes," Grandpa answered with a smile, "I *do* feel the glow, Wendell."